FROM THE MOUTH OF GOD TO MY HEART

From
THE MOUTH
of
GOD
to MY HEART

MARVIA P. PROCTOR

XULON PRESS

Xulon Press
2301 Lucien Way #415
Maitland, FL 32751
407.339.4217
www.xulonpress.com

Paperback ISBN-13: 978-1-6628-5554-2
Ebook ISBN-13: 978-1-6628-6475-9

DEDICATION

⸺⧉⸺

This book of poems is dedicated to my only son, Antonio, whose continued encouragement to finish and publish my work has finally come to pass.

INTRODUCTION

These poems were written in the early, middle, and now later stages of my adult life. God does not give us everything at one time. Fortunately, he can give us time to grow in both wisdom and understanding. My lived experience, from Arkansas to California, as a young woman and into motherhood, has connected me to people and circumstances for which I am grateful. I was blessed to expand my horizons and see that all God's children are connected no matter who or where we are. His love is all around us.

May you find a connection to some of the poems contained herein and be inspired to share your own words with the world.

God the Father, Jesus the Son

—⊶⊷—

You created this world so very long ago
Before there was a rain drop or even driven snow.
Before you placed the stars at night that gave us candlelight,
Before the hanging of the moon to give the world a glow.
Before the sea was even formed for fish to swim within,
Before you closed the greatest door
where man could stay no more.

I bet you saw this beautiful world that had no darkened sin
And could not wait to place a man so peaceful to live within.
The light from heaven would keep it bright
so man would not stumble and fall,
And yet took the greatest fall when Satan made his call.

The Earth no more will be our friend
And bring forth of its own.
Now we must labor through day and night
And build our earthly homes.
We have the sun, we have the moon,
We have the rain that falls.
But I would give it gladly back to never have taken that fall.

A Broken World

I stood upon a mountain high
looking down on a world that made me cry.
My heavenly father, what have we done
to a world that a father has given his son?

We have burned the forest that was fresh and green
And turned the earth to dust of seed.
We have taken the fields that were meant for wheat
To grow a drug we say is sweet.

We have taken the water that was fresh and clean
To bury our waste where chemicals cling.
We have taken the mountains that once stood tall
And blown them apart for just because.

We have taken the desert with the sands of time
To blow up our bombs to test our minds.
We have taken the valleys so deep and wide
To keep out a nation we have pushed aside.

This broken world is like a broken friend
When love is lost, it's hard to mend.
But God will grant us peace and time.
To mend his world and make it shine.

To God It All Belongs

Another year has come and gone
God has blessed you through it all.
We can give to you the most beautiful
flowers that man can make by hand.
We can sing to you the most beautiful
song that the ear can ever hear.

We can speak to you the kindest words,
from the mouth they spring anew.
But we can never do for you what God has done for you.
He has blessed your very soul and kept your mind at peace.
He has healed the things that lie within,
that we could never see.
He laid you down at night and let you sleep in peace.

So, on this night I say to you from each one of us
To God alone these blessings come
and to God it all belongs.

In Search of the Holy Ghost

I am searching for the Holy Ghost.
Everywhere I go, I hope to find it or it finds me.
I care not which it is to be
So long as it is found and dwells within me.

The Holy Ghost for some is a mystery.
They fear to seek that which the eyes cannot see.
But that which we see is not always what appears to be.

The Holy Ghost will always be true to you
And your mistakes so very few.
I'll take my chances on that I cannot see
And allow the Holy Ghost to keep guiding me.

If I begin to stumble and fall
The Holy Ghost will catch me, that I doubt not at all.
I would then get up and begin yet again.
'Cause you see, the Holy Ghost is truly my friend.

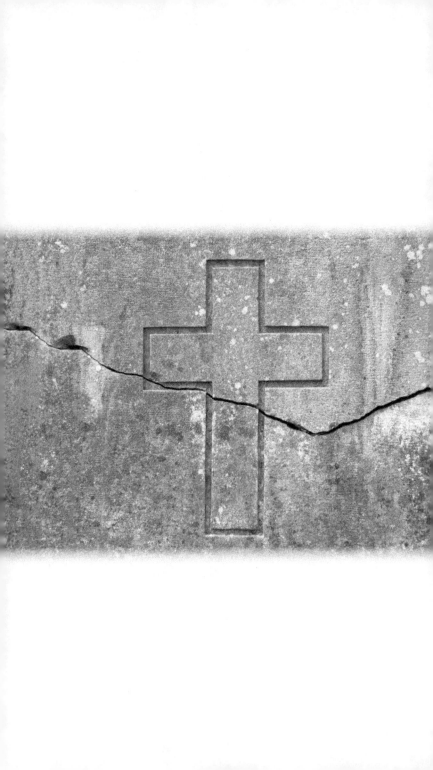

A CRACK IN THE TEMPLE, IN THE TEMPLE OF GOD

There is a crack in the temple, in the temple of God.
That crack in the temple is in the middle of our hearts.
All of the sheep are on the run
Pray to the Father through His only son.

There is a crack in the temple, in the temple of God.
The sheep are fleeing with nowhere to go.
Pray for the shepherd that his sheep may be found.
Through the crack in the temple Satan found his way.

This crack in the temple, God will surely mend.
Through the prayers of the saints, here will Satan never win.
There is a crack in the temple, please pray for us all.
We are all God's children, regardless of how we fall.

THE BLOOD OF JESUS

The blood of Jesus saved my soul.
That very same blood from the days of old.
It has healed the sick, given sight to the blind.
It has caused our race to be more loving and kind.

The blood of Jesus ran down the cross.
Every drop that hit the ground
Gave us victory and a glorious crown.
The blood of Jesus is all I need.
It keeps me at peace and on bended knee.
The blood of Jesus needs no help.
Yes, Satan has come to destroy and to kill
But because of the blood that ran down the cross,
Satan is soon to be destroyed and forever lost.

Two Roads To Travel

Some say there is a stairway to Heaven, and if it be so,
That stairway is for angels, not the men here below.
There are however two roads for men to travel upon,
The broad road to destruction where so many seem to flee.

It's neither a long journey nor hard to travel,
Just a world of destruction from which we must unravel.
There is a narrow road before us, we say it's so hard
When all God is asking is to do our own part.

At the end of this road, though it be narrow and straight
There lies a gate to enter where Jesus stands in wait.
God gave us a choice in this life which we live.
To be loving, to be kind
To be humble at all times.

It's such a small thing which he asks us to do.
Yet many will miss it because they simply choose.
But as for myself? I, who confess to love Christ
Shall stay on this narrow road the rest of my life.

Never Look Back

Never look back at yesterday,
for that lifetime has passed away.
Never look back at what could have been,
for you'll never know until life has its end.
Never look back and make yourself sad,
for life is a stage on which we must pass.
Never look back, instead pray for tomorrow.
That's one day further from any past sorrow.
So never look back, nothing can be changed.
The future can be yours, just ask in God's name.

ONE DAY AT A TIME, ONE STEP AT A TIME

—ↀↀↀ—

We worry about tomorrow, wondering if it will come
We worry about yesterday, all that's left undone.
We worry about life; how long will it be?
Knowing so well it's beyond us to see.
We worry about riches, fortune, and fame.
Knowing only through God can we seek our true aim.
One day at a time is all you should seek.
Tomorrow is not yours, let God plan your week.
One step at a time and opportunities will unfold.
The life that's before you is for more than gold.

THE BIBLE

The greatest stories that have ever been told
are stories from the Bible for saving of man's soul.
Not all are sweet, not all are kind
but it's the way God wanted to keep Heaven on our minds.
It tells of the riches that are here on earth
And how some of us are blessed from the day of our birth.
It tells of the needy, those poor from the start.
It tells us how Jesus blessed them and sanctified their hearts.
It tells of salvation and how it came to be
Of how Jesus left Heaven for you and for me.
So, let's take this book, by your side on every climb.
Love and cherish it with Jesus on your mind.
We are blessed to have it, the greatest book of all time.

A Moment is a Lifetime

It only takes a moment for the sun to rise,
For the earth to turn from side to side.

It only takes a moment for a friend to see
What a beautiful friendship lies within thee.

It only takes a moment for a kingdom to fall,
That a man spends a lifetime to build for his cause.

It only takes a moment for a child to be born,
To pass through this world within a moment unknown.
A moment is a lifetime for some, you see.
To live and to die, in a moment then become free.

WOMEN OF GOD

Women of God, do all you can.
The Lord is with you in this dying land.
Pray for your children and all of their friends,
Then pray for this world, filled with so much sin.

Women of God, He has called your name,
Not for your beauty, nor fortune nor fame,
Just to speak about Jesus and why he came.

Women of God, time is moving fast.
This earthly life was never to last.
So, sing about Him, for He is always near.
He knows your thoughts and all of your fears.

Dear women of God, pick up your cross.
Stand for Jesus who paid the cause
That we may live forever on high.
So, praise His name because he came
We have been blessed in Jesus' name.

THE FINAL SUNSET

When there is no more rain to fall
nor is destiny there to call.
When there are no more winds to blow
to clean the earth and sweep her floor.
When there are no more nights to fall
For us to sleep when slumber calls.
When there are no more stars to blink
to show our minds that we must think.
When there is no more air to breathe
to clean our bodies that are in such need.
When there is no more laughter heard
The playing of children or singing of birds
The smell of flowers or just a kind word.
Then the longest day that we shall see.
Is the falling of the sun, as it falls into the sea.
Only then are the souls, here on earth they are left
Shall they witness the falling of the final sunset.

NOTHING IS TOO HARD FOR GOD

We say this journey is long and hard
But I say this journey is just a start.
It may not be what we think it should be.
It's not in the length of time, you see.
It's neither in the labor nor the working of the hands.
It's God's way of saying, "Do all that you can."
Just live the life of a saved man,
The rest is always in God's hands.
For Jesus came and paid for it all
His love for us was worth the cause.

We say our enemy is on every side
That nowhere exists for a Christian to hide.
There's no need for a Christian to run
When a man calls Jesus, God's only son.
His blood He shed on Cavalry
has covered it all for you and me.
It is the devil, in fact, who is on the run
But he cannot hide from the Father and the Son.

We say we will be happy when this race is won.
Then we can see Jesus, God's only son.
Then do your part and do it well
So the next generation will have a story to tell.

Yes, the blood of Jesus truly paid for it all
And he is the one who will make the call.

SEVEN GOLDEN
CANDLE STICKS

Seven golden candle sticks shining bright,
Turning into angels from a distant sight.
Seven golden candle sticks burning bright,
Lighting up the heavens, oh what a beautiful sight.

Seven golden candle sticks someone called,
Leading up to heaven like a magic fall.
Seven golden candle sticks within my soul,
I know I'll get to heaven, that is my only goal.

At the End of My Rainbow

At the end of the rainbow lies a pot of gold.
At the end of the rainbow lies my very soul.
Watching and waiting for my God to call.
What a glorious day it will be for us all.
At the end of my rainbow waits a better day.
Sunshine and rain for children in which they may play
And talk to their God who is not far away.
"Come, my children", I image he would say.
"Tomorrow is the beginning of a much brighter day.
No more suffering or pain nor heartaches will be.
Your heavenly father is right here with thee."
At the end of my rainbow are mountains and hills
Facing towards the heavens, at peace, all is still.
The sky will open and angels will sing,
"Glory to God, may earth praise her king."
For he is the highest and mightiest of all.
All those who praise him will surely be called.

ONE COLD WINTER NIGHT

It happened one night so long ago,
I was sitting at my window right near my door.
The cold winter rain was falling hard.
It sounded like the world was breaking apart.

I looked at the sky, so dark and so gray.
I saw twelve little angels who wanted to play.
My heart missed a beat, out I did call,
"Please little angels, you're going to fall."
They looked at me and smiled with grace
then said to me, "we have our faith."

"Your cold winter rain is like sunshine to us,
It is in God we have all our trust."
They played about the clouds that night,
not one little angel fell from sight.
When the morning light began to come,
I heard them play a mighty drum.
"Goodbye my friend, now we must go.
Our Lord is ready to close his door."

When I Am Old

When I am old, and love is gone
The only joy will be my loving home.
Where memories will linger free
And love for life will let me be.

When I am old and cannot see
What dear sweet friend will sit with me
And tell me about the brand-new world
And how it's changed since we were girls?

When I am old and cannot walk
I'll sit and listen to the children talk
About the old that has come and gone
And about the new like the morning dew.

When I am old and cannot talk
I'll ask my Lord from within my heart
To take my soul and let it sleep.
Then take me home to rest in peace.

A MOTHER'S LOVE

There is no greater hug than a mother's hug
A special gift from God above.

There is no greater kiss than a mother's kiss
It lets me know how well I'm missed.

There is no greater smile than a mother's smile
It lets me know my life's worthwhile.

There is no greater prayer than a mother's prayer
when her child is lost out there somewhere.

There is no greater cry than a mother's cry
if she feels her child is about to die.

There is no greater peace that I can find
When mother dear is on my mind.
So, on this day I'll kneel and pray
and thank my God she's here today.

No Greater Love

A mother's love is beyond compare
There's nothing like it, not anywhere.
It rings from every mountain on high.
It brightens the heaven for all to see
It crosses the ocean that flows to the sea.

A mother's love, who could forget?
It was her love that comforted my soul,
Which sat me on the pathway for my life to unfold.

A mother's love is like a song
A melody that can never go wrong.
It soothes the mind and comforts the soul.
It puts you on a pathway that is sunny and bright
That keeps your heart singing in the still of the night.

This Mother's Day how could I forget,
You told me about life and how things would unfold.
You taught me about friendship that
was worth more than gold.
And how you would be there but not as a friend,
Rather as a mother right through till the end.

MY MOTHER'S DAY

The greatest prayer that I can pray
Is to thank my God for this Mother's Day.

I am standing here and smiling bright,
My mother's face, a beautiful sight.

She smiles at me when I'm asleep
And says in me she finds her peace.

There will never been a better day
than Mother's Day to pass this way.

And when this Mother's Day has an end,
I know I have no better friend.

SOMEBODY'S CHILD

The streets are cold and dark at night.
Someone's child is in a fright.
No place to run. No place to hide.
Please, dear God, stand by his side.
He's left alone as if by dare,
Not one good friend who seems to care.

I saw him kneel and pray today.
He asked his God to make a way.
To free him from this world with care,
to find some happiness over there.
I heard him say, "My Lord, I pray.
I need your help, your help today."

"I never had a mother's love
to teach me of your book above.
I never had a mother's smile
to show me life can be worthwhile.
But with your love and with your grace,
I'll try to keep up with this race.
And when my time shall be no more,
I ask of thee to close the door."

CHILDREN OF CONFUSION

Children are sweet, children are kind.
We as adults can make them so blind.
Twisting and turning their little minds.
Trying to make them like our mankind.
We lift their spirits and kiss them with joy,
Then turn and treat them like a broken toy.
We take their daylight and turn it into night,
Then rake their minds of any good that's in sight.
We tell them there is peace if they'll be good,
That God will grant them a lovely childhood.
Sweet little children,
they look up to us and believe what we say.
Yet it is we who've lost ourselves along the way.
I'm grateful there's a God who watches from above,
Who watches over his children and showers them with love.

LITTLE CHILDREN FROM ACROSS THE SEA

Sweet little children from across the sea,
Dreaming of America, they say she is free.
A land with sunshine and freedom to play,
A land that is blessed through time of night and day.

Sweet little children from across the sea,
Our America is not always so free.
Our little children are dying here too.
Only God and faith can pull them through.
Stay in your land, it's just as free.
Ask God to bless it and you will see.

FRESH AND CLEAN

⸻

The soul of a child is like the morning rain
Fresh and clean like the beginning of spring.
I often wonder why must a child die.
Does God need their souls to light up the sky?
To let us know there is beauty on the earth
And it all began from the day of our birth?

A WARM SUMMER NIGHT

One warm summer night the earth stood still.
No life around me that I could feel.
I started to cry when I heard a voice
call my name and touch my heart.
Your world is old; it needs to rest.
It has stood many a test.

It has rolled around many years,
Shed for many its rainy tears.
It has held the floods, calmed the seas,
Brought the wind to bended knees.
It has fought the night until the day,
Yet always seems to find its way.
It will turn again when it is time.
Just let it sleep and find its peace.

THE BOTTOMLESS SEA

The sea is deep, so deep and wide.
I often wonder what lives inside.
I know there are fish. I know there are whales.
I know there are sharks with stories to tell.
But what lies beneath the cold, cold deep
where only our God has walked beneath?

The water is cold and black as night.
I'd bet only angels can see the light.
The moon and the stars dance above
then shine on the water as if in love.
The waves run across the sea at night
and trouble the water as if there were light.

The wind and the rain come down so hard.
It sings to the water to be on guard.
Of broken ships and broken planes
that fills its body with souls of pain.
Oh, water of the deep, oh, water of the night
With no endless bottom or light in sight.
One day this world will surely be told
of all the mysteries your bottom holds.

COME OUT OF THE DARKNESS

The light beheld the beauty for all the world to see.
Yet half is only make-believe to draw out you and me.

Yet when the night begins to fall and
darkness covers the land,
That's when the evil ones come out
and take your little hands.

He will lead you down a path where light is never found.
He will take away your childhood,
Your golden smiles and frowns.

He will set you in the darkest pit and tell you no one cares.
You are just another boy and girl,
In a world that does not care.

But there are many in this world who truly understand.
Just reach out your little hands
And let us take ahold
Then pull you from the darkest night that has a deadly hold.

We will pray to him who lives on high
That watches you from the sky.
To bring you to the light again and keep you safe within.

Then you can tell the others to come out of the night
And trust the ones who are reaching
out with God-given light.
Now watch him keep you safe at
night and always in his sight.

No Reflection of Me

I looked in my mirror on a solid wall.
No reflection of me. No reflection at all.
I turned around to find myself,
My reflection had taken another step.
Around the room it danced about
and left my mind without a doubt.

Reflection of me, you must not go.
Please come and dance within my door.
Upon my wall you must jump about,
into my mirror without a doubt.
Now I know just who I am.
My reflection I see, I know is me.

MOVING ON

I live in a world that is not so kind.
But back as a child I made up my mind
To learn all I can, to take my stand,
I will not stop to think whether I can.

I am old enough to know what is right.
You see, my mother kept that in sight.
I shall not put away my buttons and bows.
They are the link to my youth and to small stories untold.

I shall not forget to still run and to play,
Yet get back to my home by the end of the day.

I shall not forget to say "thanks" and "please".
I will never be too old for any of these.

I want only to keep growing and becoming wiser each day,
So that I may help others along their way.

I will stay in school; that's my first golden rule.
The rest will come as I grow.
I want to be ready for life when it opens the door.

MY PUZZLE OF LIFE

There is a puzzle to our life
I was once told.
Try to put it together
And see what life holds.
So many pieces all scattered about.
I look at my puzzle, I see no way out.
Slowly, the Master took my hand.
He gathered the pieces together so I could understand.
He placed a piece here, He laid a piece there.
My Lord, I have brothers and sisters out there.
The puzzle began to take on its shape.
I knew then He had opened the gate.
I picked up your piece, snapped it right in.
I knew I had found you, my sister, my friend.
My puzzle of life, now nearly connected in place.
I'm glad part of it holds your beautiful face.
I know not what nor where the end will be,
For my brothers, my sisters, nor even for me.
But there's one thing I want you know:
When all the parts are snapped into place,
There will be no greater part
than your beautiful face.

The Hands of Death

The hands of death are dark and cold.
It comes alone to take your soul.
It walks the land and treads the seas.
It calls your name without a please.
It searches the days as well as the nights
To let you know it's right in sight.
It cares not what your race may be.
It wants your soul, then it flees.
Across the water from whence it came
Till time has come to search again.

TODAY AND FOREVER

—∞∞∞—

Today is the beginning of my brand-new life
I have opened my heart and accepted dear Christ.
Today is the beginning for all to see
The brand-new person I found within me.
Today is the beginning for my heart to seek,
my salvation, to set my soul free.
Today and forever, so long as there's life
I will place all my hopes and trust in you, dear Christ.

My Today Is My Tomorrow

I shall live my tomorrow for today,
in case, tomorrow I shall pass away.
I shall live my tomorrow with laughter and play,
you see, my tomorrow began today.
I shall live my tomorrow with my Lord today.
He never promised me tomorrow, nor all of this day.
I shall live my tomorrow trying to do right.
You see, my tomorrow might end tonight.
I shall live my tomorrow not trying to impress,
You see, not one living soul can pass all of God's test.
I shall live my tomorrow at the beginning of each day
So, if there is no tomorrow, my soul will find peace
Knowing that tomorrow, we all could be sleep.

ACKNOWLEDGEMENTS

- To all my family and friends over the decades who read or accepted a poem and encouraged me to write more, I thank you.

- To my deceased but never forgotten sister, Jannie A. Young.

- To my son and greatest encouragement, Antonio, for his editing eye and typing touch.

THE AUTHOR

M s. Proctor is a mother to her son, a daughter, a sister to nine siblings, a friend, auntie, godmother, and child of God who lives to spread the word of Christ by using the poetic skill with which she is blessed. She was born in the small town of Fordyce, Arkansas, to Miss Francis C. Hall, who too was a writer but never published her work. "I am grateful to be able to share this inherited ability."

CPSIA information can be obtained
at www.ICGtesting.com
Printed in the USA
BVHW070050040123
655456BV00008B/600

9 781662 855542